BLUE Prints

For School Guidance and Counseling (K-12)

A Comprehensive Assortment
of Professionally Designed
Black-Line Masters

Includes More Than 160
Forms and Letters:

- Needs Assessments
- Bulletin Board Ideas
- Public Relations Documents
- Small Group and Classroom Guidance
- Parent Conferences and Consultations
- Data Collection & Accountability
- Thank You Letters
- And Much More!

by Ronald D. Miles, Ph.D., LPC

youth light
inc.

© 2005 by YouthLight, Inc.
Chapin, SC 29036

Cover Design by Amy Rule
Design and Layout by Diane Florence • Project Editing by Bob Bowman

ISBN
1889636991

Library of Congress Number
2005927218

Printed in the United Staes

Dedication

To Chris, you'll always be in my heart.

Acknowledgements

To Susan and Bob Bowman for once again encouraging and supporting my work.

To the many incredible school counselors who make a difference in the lives of people every day.

To God for blessing my life with creativity and commitment.

About the Author

Dr. Ronald D. Miles is an educational consultant, college instructor, author and Licensed Professional Counselor. With over thirty-three years experience as an educator, he has served in the area of school counseling for twenty years. As an elementary school counselor, his program was recognized nationally and was featured in the text The Best For Our Kids. As a district level Guidance Director, his program was selected as one of ten nationally recognized guidance and counseling programs and has been featured in two major guidance texts. Dr. Miles has been selected as "South Carolina Counselor of the Year" and as The American School Counselor Association's "National Guidance Administrator of the Year."

Overview of the Book

Blueprints for School Guidance and Counseling is a three part series designed to assist the school counselor with user friendly and reproducible forms and letters for effective program management. Although each part can be used separately, it is suggested that all components be incorporated into a comprehensive developmental guidance and counseling program in order to assure greater success. An overview of each of the three parts follows.

- Needs Assessments
- Program Planning
- Outreach
- Data Collection and Accountability

- Referral Forms
- Appointment Reminders
- Small Group Guidance and Counseling Procedures
- Classroom Guidance Procedures
- Parent Conferences and Consultation Procedures
- Intervention Management Techniques

- Affirmations
- Thank You Letters
- Reference Letters
- Public Relations Documents
- Bulletin Board Ideas

PART ONE: BUILDING A SOLID FOUNDATION

Overview

An effective school guidance and counseling program is based on a solid foundation that includes developmental and proactive strategies that address the individual and group needs of students, parents and guardians, educational colleagues, and the community as a whole. Part One will assist the school counselor with resources and techniques that will create this foundation. It is divided into four sections. They are as follows.

- Needs Assessments
- Program Planning
- Outreach
- Data Collection and Accountability

Once a solid foundation is developed, the school counselor will become better equipped to communicate information in regards to guidance and counseling initiatives, activities, events, and program outcomes. This, in turn, will enhance positive public relations as well as school and community support.

TABLE OF CONTENTS

TABLE OF CONTENTS

SECTION ONE:
NEEDS ASSESSMENTS

This section provides practical strategies for assisting the school counselor with the identification of school and community needs as they relate to a comprehensive and developmental school guidance and counseling program. Included are assessments for students, educational colleagues, parents and guardians, and the community. With the identification of "customer" needs, it is important to recall the words from the film *Field of Dreams,* "If you build the field, they will come." A school guidance and counseling program that both identifies and addresses school and community needs is definitely one that has built the field.

Name _____

1. This is a picture of how I feel when I am at school.

2. This is a picture of how I feel when I am not at school.

3. This is a picture of me with my friends.

4. This is a picture of me with my family.

5. This is a picture of something I enjoy doing.

Name _____

Teacher _____

Please place an "X" beside the things you would like to learn more about this school year.

- ☐ Making and Keeping Friends
- ☐ Doing My Best at School
- ☐ Getting Along With My Brother or Sister
- ☐ Being Safe
- ☐ Feeling Good About Myself
- ☐ Work, Jobs, and Careers
- ☐ Thing to Do When I Am Bored
- ☐ Ways to Help My School and Community
- ☐ Being Helpful at Home
- ☐ Dealing With Bullies
- ☐ Moving – Getting to Know a New School and Neighborhood
- ☐ What to Do When Someone or Something Dies
- ☐ How to Handle My Feelings
- ☐ Being Healthy
- ☐ Other People and Countries
- ☐ Community Helpers

What are some other things that you would like to learn more about?

_____

_____

_____

Name _____

Teacher _____

Please place an "X" beside the small groups you would like to attend this school year.

- [ ] Being A New Student at This School
- [ ] Making and Keeping Friends
- [ ] Understanding Family Changes – Divorce
- [ ] Understanding Family Changes – New Family Members
- [ ] Handling My Feelings When I Get Upset
- [ ] What Do I Do When Someone Dies
- [ ] Doing My Best With School Work and Tests

What are some other groups that you would like to attend?

_____

_____

_____

_____

_____

Name _____

Teacher _____

1. What are some words that would describe how you feel at school?

   _____

2. What are some words that describe how you feel when you are not at school?

   _____

3. What are the first names of your friends?

   _____

4. What are some things that you enjoy?

   _____

5. What makes you feel happy?

   _____

6. What makes you feel angry?

   _____

7. What makes you feel confused?

   _____

8. What makes you feel afraid?

   _____

9. What things do you like about yourself?

   _____

Name _____

Teacher _____

During this school year, we will learn about many things in classroom guidance sessions. To help prepare for these sessions, please place an "X" beside the topics about which you would like to learn more.

❏ Understanding Who I Am

❏ Making and Keeping Friends

❏ Learning About Different People and Cultures

❏ Understanding Death and Loss

❏ Resolving Conflicts

❏ Being Successful at School

❏ Homework and Tests

❏ What I Want to Be When I Grow Up

❏ Ways to Help My Community

❏ Being Safe and Healthy

What are some other things that you would like to learn about this school year?

_____

_____

_____

SMALL GROUP GUIDANCE & COUNSELING

Name _____

Teacher _____

During this school year, students will be invited to participate in small groups in which they will learn more about a topic of personal interest. In order to identify groups that may be of interest to you, please place an "X" beside your choices from the list below.

❑ Being Successful in School

❑ Studying and Test Taking

❑ Being a Friend

❑ Being A New Student at This School

❑ Learning About Ways to Help My Community

❑ Becoming a Peer Helper

❑ Understanding Family Changes – Divorce

❑ Understanding Family Changes – New Family Members

❑ Dealing With Loss and Grief

❑ Understanding and Coping With Anger

❑ Dealing With Bullies and Teasing

What are the names of other small groups that are of interest to you?

_____

_____

_____

STUDENT NEEDS ASSESSMENT GRADES 6-8
CLASSROOM GUIDANCE

Name _____

Teacher _____

During this school year we will explore many subjects of interest to middle school students through our classroom guidance program. In order to plan for this program, please place an "X" beside the subjects that you would like to discuss during classroom guidance sessions.

- ☐ Understanding Middle School Life
- ☐ Getting to Know Myself Better
- ☐ Dealing With Changes in Relationships
- ☐ Making Friends
- ☐ Understanding Different People and Cultures
- ☐ Taking Notes, Studying, and Test Taking
- ☐ Successful Work Habits
- ☐ Work and Careers
- ☐ Dealing With Peer Pressure
- ☐ Making Safe and Responsible Choices
- ☐ Understanding Changes in My Body
- ☐ Preparing for High School
- ☐ Community Volunteer Opportunities

What are some other subjects that you would like to discuss during classroom guidance sessions?

_____

_____

_____

SMALL GROUP GUIDANCE & COUNSELING

Name _____

Teacher _____

Students in our school have the opportunity to choose to participate in small groups that address individual or group issues and concerns. In order to select the types of groups that are of interest to the students in our school, please place an "X" beside the groups that are of interest to you.

- ☐ Being a New Student at This School
- ☐ Learning About Successful School Habits
- ☐ Dealing With Conflict and Anger
- ☐ What to Do When We "Break Up"
- ☐ Skills in Friendship Development
- ☐ Coping With My Parents' Divorce
- ☐ Dealing With Brothers and Sisters
- ☐ Being Part of a Blended Family
- ☐ Understanding Who I Am
- ☐ Becoming a Peer Helper
- ☐ Service Learning

What are some other groups that may interest you?

_____

_____

_____

_____

Name _____

Teacher _____

During the school year we will discuss topics of interest to high school students during scheduled guidance sessions. In order to make these sessions helpful to you, please take a few minutes and complete the following needs assessment. Your assistance is appreciated.

1. What are some of the major challenges that confront students in our school?

     _____

     _____

2. What are the major academic hurdles that you face at school? _____

     _____

     _____

3. What are some issues and concerns that you would like to discuss during classroom guidance sessions? _____

     _____

     _____

4. How can the guidance program at our school better assist you with academic, career, personal, or social concerns? _____

     _____

     _____

5. What topics would you like to explore in regards to your plans after high school graduation? _____

     _____

     _____

6. Do you have any additional comments regarding our guidance program? _____
     If so, what are they? _____

     _____

Name _____

Teacher _____

Throughout the school year students will be invited to participate in small guidance and counseling groups at our school. Participation is strictly voluntary. In order to identify groups that may interest our students, your input is needed. Please take a few minutes to complete the following checklist of groups that may be of personal interest to you. Your assistance is appreciated.

I am interested in the following groups.

☐ Improving My Grades

☐ Dealing With Personal Relationships

☐ Preparing for Life After Graduation

☐ Handling Peer Pressure

☐ Getting Along With My Family Members

☐ Exploring My Career Options

☐ Coping With College Life

☐ Becoming a Peer Helper

☐ Dating: Sometimes It Makes Me Crazy

What are the topics of other groups that are of interest to you?

_____
_____
_____
_____
_____

In order to develop a comprehensive developmental guidance program that addresses the needs of our students, your insights and feelings are very important. Please take a few minutes to complete the following needs assessment. Your help is sincerely appreciated.

Name _____ Grade _____

1. What do feel are the major challenges to the students in our school? How do you think we can address these challenges? _____

   _____

   _____

2. How can the guidance and counseling program in our school assist you with your work as an educator?

   _____

   _____

3. What topics would you like to see addressed in classroom guidance sessions?

   _____

   _____

4. Small group guidance and counseling in our school needs to address the following topics.

   _____

   _____

5. Parents and guardians in our school are in need of the following programs, services, or resources.

   _____

   _____

6. I would like to be involved in the guidance program in the following ways.

   ❏ Using classroom guidance enrichment activities
   ❏ Serving on a guidance committee
   ❏ Serving as student mentor or tutor
   ❏ Assisting with a guidance program event or activity
   ❏ Presenting a faculty or parent/guardian workshop
   ❏ Other ideas, please list _____

7. Please share any additional comments in reference to our school's guidance and counseling program.

   _____

   _____

As part of an on-going effort to provide a necessary and appropriate guidance and counseling program, your help is needed. Please take a few minutes to respond to the following questions and statements. Your responses will assist our school in addressing the guidance and counseling needs of our students, parents and guardians, community, and school staff. Thank you for your time.

Name _____ Grade _____

1. Middle school has often been described as a time of great transition for young people. What do see as the major transition issues that confront our students? How can we address these issues?

   _____

   _____

   _____

2. Parental involvement is a key element for student success in school. How can the guidance and counseling program increase parental involvement at our school? _____

   _____

   _____

3. What topics would you like to see addressed in our school's classroom guidance program?

   _____

   _____

4. Small counseling groups that are needed by our students include the following.

   _____

   _____

5. What guidance consultation services would assist you in your role as an educator?

   _____

   _____

   _____

6. What additional strategies, suggestions, or comments do you have in regards to our school's guidance and counseling program? _____

   _____

   _____

7. What are some ways that you can assist with the guidance and counseling program? Check those that apply.

   ❑ Assist with a guidance activity or event   ❑ Others, please list
   ❑ Serve on a guidance committee   _____
   ❑ Serve as a student mentor or tutor
   ❑ Use follow-up enrichment activities related   _____
     to classroom guidance
   ❑ Conduct a parent/guardian or faculty   _____
     workshop

As the students in our high school prepare for their academic, career, and personal futures, it is important that they receive the necessary guidance in making personally appropriate decisions. A proactive, comprehensive, and developmental guidance and counseling program can assist with this endeavor. Therefore, in order to provide the necessary program components, your assistance is needed. Please take a few minutes to respond to this needs assessment. Your wisdom is sincerely appreciated.

Name _____ Grade _____

1. High school students are faced with many challenges as they prepare for their post-secondary lives. What do feel are the major challenges that confront today's high school students? How can we as high school educators assist our students with these challenges? _____
    _____
    _____

2. How can our school's guidance and counseling program assist students and parents/guardians with educational and career decisions? _____
    _____
    _____

3. What materials and resources would you like to see available in the school's guidance center?
    _____
    _____

4. What topics and issues would you like to see addressed in our school's classroom guidance sessions?
    _____
    _____

5. What types of individual and small group counseling services are needed by our students?
    _____
    _____
    _____

6. What guidance consultation services would assist you in your role as an educator?
    _____
    _____
    _____

7. Do you have additional suggestions or comments in reference to our school's guidance and counseling program? If so, please list those here. _____
    _____
    _____
    _____
    _____
    _____

As part of providing a comprehensive developmental guidance and counseling program for our school, your help as a primary caregiver for our students is very important. Please assist us in providing the best program for you and your child(ren) by responding to the following questions and statements. Should you have any questions, please contact our school counselor, _____, at _____. Your assistance is appreciated.

1. How can our school's guidance and counseling program assist you and your child(ren) in the following areas?

    A. **School and Academic Success** _____
    _____
    _____

    B. **Peer Relationships** _____
    _____
    _____

    C. **Self Concept** _____
    _____
    _____

    D. **Family Concerns** _____
    _____
    _____

    E. **Community Issues** _____
    _____
    _____

    F. **Health and Safety** _____
    _____
    _____

2. What resources and materials do you need from the school's guidance center?
    _____
    _____
    _____
    _____

3. What are your suggestions for workshops for parents and guardians? When would be the best days and times to offer these workshops? _____

_____

_____

_____

4. What guidance consultation services would be helpful for your family?

_____

_____

_____

_____

5. What other suggestions or comments do you have in regards to our school's guidance and counseling program? _____

_____

_____

_____

6. Would you be interest in being a guidance volunteer? If so, please check those that apply.

   ❑ Serving as a student mentor
   ❑ Serving as a student tutor
   ❑ Assisting with a guidance event or activity
   ❑ Serving on a guidance committee
   ❑ Other ideas, please list_____

_____

_____

Name _____   Child's Name _____

Telephone Number _____

MIDDLE SCHOOL

In an effort to define, expand, and enrich the comprehensive developmental guidance and counseling program at our school, your assistance as a parent and/or guardian is extremely important. Please take a few minutes and complete the following needs assessment. Your comments will be help us in providing the best program for you and your child(ren). If you have any questions, please contact our school counselor, _____, at _____. Your assistance is appreciated.

1. What do you feel are the major needs of middle school students? How can our school assist you in addressing these needs? _____

   _____

   _____

   _____

2. How can the guidance and counseling program assist your child(ren) in achieving success in school? _____

   _____

   _____

   _____

3. What guidance consultation services would be helpful for you and your family?

   _____

   _____

   _____

   _____

4. What transition support services can the guidance and counseling program provide for your child(ren) in the following areas?

   A. Entering middle school   _____

   _____

   B. Preparing for high school   _____

   _____

   C. Handling peer pressure   _____

   _____

   D. Dealing with family changes   _____

   _____

5. What materials and resources should be available for families in the school's guidance center? _____

_____

_____

_____

6. What other comments or suggestions do you have for our school's guidance and counseling program?

_____

_____

_____

7. Would you be interested in serving as a guidance volunteer? If so, please check all that apply.
   ❏ Serving as a student mentor
   ❏ Serving as a student tutor
   ❏ Assisting with a guidance event or activity
   ❏ Serving on a guidance committee
   ❏ Speaking to students about your career
   ❏ Others, please list_____

_____

_____

Name _____   Child's Name _____

Telephone Number _____

The years spent in high school are years of critical importance for our young men and women as they approach their lives as adults. It is strategically important that our students receive the necessary guidance and support during these important years of development. Please assist us in identifying the needs of our students and their families as we work together with the implementation of a comprehensive developmental guidance and counseling program. Thank you for taking the time to respond to the following items. Please contact our school counselor, _____, at _____ should you have any questions.

1. Does your child(ren) have any academic needs or concerns? If so, how would you describe them?

   _____

   _____

   _____

   _____

2. How can our school's guidance and counseling program address the academic needs of your child(ren)?

   _____

   _____

   _____

   _____

3. How can our school's guidance and counseling program address the post-secondary and career needs of your child(ren)? _____

   _____

   _____

   _____

4. Do our school and community have a negative peer pressure problem? If so, how can we address this issue? _____

   _____

   _____

   _____

5. Are there concerns you have regarding your child's safety? If so, how can our school and community work together to assure that all children are safe? _____

   _____

   _____

   _____

6. What guidance consultation services would be beneficial to you and your family?

_____

_____

_____

_____

7. What materials and resources need to be available for families in our school's guidance center?

_____

_____

_____

_____

8. What additional comments or suggestions do you have in reference to our school's guidance and counseling program? _____

_____

_____

_____

9. Would you like to be a guidance program volunteer? If so, check those that apply.
   - ❏ Serve as a career speaker
   - ❏ Assist with a guidance event or activity
   - ❏ Serve as a student mentor
   - ❏ Serve as a student tutor
   - ❏ Assist with a guidance committee
   - ❏ Others, please list _____

_____

_____

_____

Name _____ Child's Name _____

Telephone Number _____

COMMUNITY GROUP NEEDS ASSESSMENT

In an effort to provide a comprehensive guidance and counseling program for the students in our school, it is important that effective community partnerships be created with agencies, the faith community, and other civic and/or community groups. Combining efforts we can assist our students and their families with programs and services that address personal, social, career, and academic needs. Please join us in this process by taking a few minutes to complete the following needs assessment. Should you have any questions, please contact our school counselor, _____, at _____.Your assistance is sincerely appreciated.

Name of Agency or Community Group _____

Address _____

Telephone   Person Completing
Number: _____   Needs Assessment: _____

1. What does your group view as the major concerns of young people today? How has your group attempted to address these concerns? _____

_____

_____

_____

_____

2. What can the schools do to address these concerns? _____

_____

_____

_____

_____

3. To what degree are you aware of your local school's guidance and counseling program? Would you like additional information about this program? _____

_____

_____

_____

_____

4. How can our school's guidance and counseling program work with your group to address common issues and concerns among young people? _____

_____

_____

_____

_____

5. Would your group be interested in volunteer opportunities within the guidance and counseling program? If so, please check those that may apply.

   ❏ Student Mentor
   ❏ Student Tutor
   ❏ Assisting With a Guidance Event or Activity
   ❏ Serving on a Guidance Committee
   ❏ Providing Materials and Resources
   ❏ Others, please list _____

_____

_____

_____

_____

6. Do you have any questions, comments, or suggestions in regards to our school's guidance and counseling program? _____

_____

_____

_____

_____

COMMUNITY MEMBER NEEDS ASSESSMENT

Thank you for your interest in our school's guidance and counseling program. Working together we can provide the best programs and services for all of our students. Your time and talent are deeply appreciated. In order to assist us enriching our guidance and counseling program, please take a few minutes to complete this needs assessment. Should you have any questions, contact our school counselor, _____ at _____. Your assistance is appreciated.

Name _____ Telephone Number _____

Address _____

1. What do you consider are the needs of today's young people? What can the schools do to address these needs? _____

   _____

   _____

   _____

2. To what degree are you aware of your local school's guidance and counseling program? Would you like to receive more information about this program? _____

   _____

   _____

   _____

3. What materials, resources, and services do you see as critical to the success of a school's guidance and counseling program? _____

   _____

   _____

   _____

   _____

4. Do you have any additional questions, comments, or suggestions in regards to school guidance and counseling? _____

_____

_____

_____

_____

5. Would you be interested in becoming a volunteer with the guidance and counseling program? If so, check those that apply.

❑ Student Mentor
❑ Student Tutor
❑ Serving on a Guidance Committee
❑ Assisting With a Guidance Activity or Event
❑ Serving as a Career Speaker
❑ Others, please list _____

_____

_____

_____

_____

_____

_____

SECTION TWO:
PROGRAM PLANNING

Once the needs of students, parents and guardians, educational colleagues, and the community are identified, the school counselor is ready to organize this valuable data. An effective school guidance and counseling program is based on professional planning that reflects the needs of a school and its community. Section Two provides the counselor with ready-to-use forms for long and short range planning. Emphasis is placed on the inclusion of National Standards for school counseling along with curriculum coordination. As was once stated, "the best offense is a good defense." Certainly necessary and professionally based program planning is that "good defense" that counselors need.

Based on the results of the school's guidance and counseling program needs assessments the following summary results have been identified.

STUDENTS

Classroom Guidance Needs

1. _____
2. _____
3. _____
4. _____
5. _____
6. _____
7. _____
8. _____
9. _____
10. _____

Small Group Guidance and Counseling

1. _____
2. _____
3. _____
4. _____
5. _____
6. _____
7. _____
8. _____
9. _____
10. _____

EDUCATIONAL COLLEAGUES

Classroom Guidance

1. _____
2. _____
3. _____
4. _____
5. _____
6. _____
7. _____
8. _____
9. _____
10. _____

EDUCATIONAL COLLEAGUES

Small Group Guidance and Counseling

1. _____
2. _____
3. _____
4. _____
5. _____
6. _____
7. _____
8. _____
9. _____
10. _____

Resources Needed

1. _____
2. _____
3. _____
4. _____
5. _____
6. _____
7. _____
8. _____
9. _____
10. _____

Consultation Services Needed

1. _____
2. _____
3. _____
4. _____
5. _____
6. _____
7. _____
8. _____
9. _____
10. _____

PARENTS AND GUARDIANS

Student Needs

1. _____
2. _____
3. _____
4. _____
5. _____
6. _____
7. _____
8. _____
9. _____
10. _____

Resources Needed

1. _____
2. _____
3. _____
4. _____
5. _____
6. _____
7. _____
8. _____
9. _____
10. _____

Consultation Services Needed

1. _____
2. _____
3. _____
4. _____
5. _____
6. _____
7. _____
8. _____
9. _____
10. _____

Desired Workshops

1. _____   6. _____
2. _____   7. _____
3. _____   8. _____
4. _____   9. _____
5. _____   10. _____

COMMUNITY GROUPS AND MEMBERS

Program Needs

1. _____
2. _____
3. _____
4. _____
5. _____
6. _____
7. _____
8. _____
9. _____
10. _____

Available Community Resources and Partnerships

1. _____
2. _____
3. _____
4. _____
5. _____
6. _____
7. _____
8. _____
9. _____
10. _____

SUMMARY FINDINGS

Common Needs for All Groups

1. _____
2. _____
3. _____
4. _____
5. _____
6. _____
7. _____
8. _____
9. _____
10. _____

Once school and community guidance and counseling needs have been compiled and summarized, the next step is to align the needs with The National Guidance Curriculum Standards for Student Development. Under each of the following standards, the school counselor will list the identified needs.

LEARNING TO LIVE

1. Students will understand and appreciate self.

2. Students will understand and respect others.

3. Students will understand and appreciate home and family.

4. Students will develop a sense of community.

5. Students will make decisions, set goals, and take actions.

6. Students will develop safety and survival skills.

LEARNING TO LEARN

1. Students will develop personal qualities that contribute to being an effective learner.

2. Students will employ strategies to achieve school success.

3. Students will understand the interrelationship of life in the school, home, community, and society.

LEARNING TO WORK

1. Students will understand the relationships among personal qualities, education and training, and the world of work.

2. Students will demonstrate decision-making, goal-setting, problem-solving and communication skills.

3. Students will explore careers and the connection of school to work.

4. Students will demonstrate a positive attitude toward work and the ability to work together.

5. Students will understand how community awareness relates to work.

QUESTIONS FOR REFLECTION AND PLANNING

1. How closely are our school and community needs aligned with the national standards?

2. Do our school and community have needs that are not addressed by the national standards?

3. Are there national standards that have not been identified as needs by my school and community?

4. How can I relate theses findings to members of my school and community?

PROGRAM PLANNING LONG RANGE PLANNING

After identified needs are correlated to The National Guidance Curriculum Standards for Student Development, the long-range program planning process is necessary to assure that all standards and needs are addressed during the school year. The following frameworks can be used as a long-range planning guide.

FRAMEWORK ONE

National Standard	Student Competency	School Need	Counselor Strategy

PROGRAM PLANNING LONG RANGE PLANNING

After identified needs are correlated to The National Guidance Curriculum Standards for Student Development, the long-range program planning process is necessary to assure that all standards and needs are addressed during the school year. The following frameworks can be used as a long-range planning guide.

FRAMEWORK TWO

Counselor Strategy	Resources Needed	Curriculum Correlation*	Date

* The curriculum correlation refers to the school subject area or standard that relates to the counselor strategy.

Title of Unit _____

Grade Levels _____

Standards Addressed _____

_____

_____

_____

_____

Student Competencies Addressed _____

_____

_____

_____

_____

Subject Area/Standards Correlation _____

_____

_____

_____

_____

Session Topics

1. _____

2. _____

3. _____

4. _____

5. _____

6. _____

7. _____

8. _____

9. _____

10. _____

Materials and Resources Needed _____

_____

_____

Duration of Unit (Time Allocations) _____

_____

Desired Outcomes

1. _____
2. _____
3. _____
4. _____
5. _____
6. _____
7. _____
8. _____
9. _____
10. _____

Methods of Assessment

1. _____
2. _____
3. _____
4. _____
5. _____
6. _____
7. _____
8. _____
9. _____
10. _____

Title of Session _____

Grade Levels _____

Time Allocation _____

Standards Addressed

1. _____

2. _____

3. _____

4. _____

5. _____

Student Competencies Addressed

1. _____

2. _____

3. _____

4. _____

5. _____

6. _____

7. _____

8. _____

9. _____

10. _____

Subject Areas/Standards Correlation

1. _____

2. _____

3. _____

4. _____

5. _____

PROGRAM PLANNING – SHORT RANGE CLASSROOM GUIDANCE SESSION

Materials and Resources Needed

Session Outline

Introduction

Participation and Process Activities

Closure

Follow-up

Desired Outcomes

1.
2.
3.
4.
5.
6.
7.
8.
9.
10.

Methods of Assessment

1.
2.
3.
4.
5.

PROGRAM PLANNING – SHORT RANGE SMALL GROUP PLAN

Title of Group _____

Age and/or Grade Levels _____

Time Allocations _____

Identified Student Needs

1. _____
2. _____
3. _____
4. _____
5. _____
6. _____
7. _____
8. _____

Legal and/or Ethical Considerations

1. _____
2. _____
3. _____
4. _____
5. _____

Session Topics

1. _____
2. _____
3. _____
4. _____
5. _____
6. _____
7. _____
8. _____

© YouthLight, Inc.

Follow-up Strategies

1. _____
2. _____
3. _____
4. _____
5. _____
6. _____
7. _____
8. _____

Materials and Resources Needed _____
_____

Desired Outcomes

1. _____
2. _____
3. _____
4. _____
5. _____
6. _____
7. _____
8. _____

Methods of Assessment

1. _____
2. _____
3. _____
4. _____
5. _____

Title of Session _____

Age and/or Grade Levels _____

Time Allocation _____

Legal and/or Ethical Considerations

    1. _____

    2. _____

    3. _____

    4. _____

    5. _____

Session Outline

  Opening _____

_____

  Ice Breaker *(if needed)* _____

_____

  Review Issues *(if needed)* _____

_____

  Session Activites _____

_____

  Discussion and Proceeding of Activities _____

_____

  Closure and Follow-up _____

_____

Materials and Resources Needed _____

_____

_____

Desired Outcomes

1. _____

2. _____

3. _____

4. _____

5. _____

6. _____

7. _____

8. _____

9. _____

10. _____

Methods of Assessment

1. _____

2. _____

3. _____

4. _____

5. _____

6. _____

7. _____

8. _____

9. _____

10. _____

PROGRAM PLANNING – SHORT RANGE
FACULTY OR PARENT WORKSHOP

Title of Workshop _____

Target Audience _____

Description of Workshop (Needs Addressed) _____

_____

_____

Time Allocation _____

Methods of Promotion or Recruitment

    1. _____

    2. _____

    3. _____

    4. _____

    5. _____

Materials and Resources Needed _____

_____

_____

Special Group Considerations _____

_____

_____

_____

_____

_____

Program Outline

Introduction

Ice Breaker *(if needed)*

Program Content or Activites

Questions and Discussion

Closing

Follow-up

Desired Outcomes

1.

2.

3.

4.

5.

Methods of Assessment

1.

2.

3.

4.

5.

SECTION THREE:
OUTREACH

Once needs assessments' results, national standards and related subject area curricula are correlated into a comprehensive long range plan, the effective school counselor is only steps away from program implementation. The first of these important steps is to reconnect with members of the school and community in order to generate awareness regarding identified needs along with program plans and anticipated outcomes. This endeavor is often referred to as "outreach." Section Three provides the school counselor with outreach forms for parents and guardians, students, educational colleagues, and the community. Both long and short range program initiatives are addressed.

GUIDANCE NEWS
FOR PARENTS AND GUARDIANS

Dear Parents and Guardians,

Thank you for your recent responses to our school's Guidance and Counseling Program Needs Assessment. Your comments and suggestions have proven to be a valuable component in designing our school-wide comprehensive developmental guidance and counseling program. Combining your needs with those expressed by our students, educators, and community members, our school's program has been strengthened as an integral part of our total educational plan.

Listed below are the summary results of our needs assessment along with an overview of our guidance and counseling program for this school year. Please contact me should you have any questions. Your support is appreciated.

Sincerely,

School Counselor

NEEDS ASSESSMENTS' RESULTS

Parents and Guardians

1. _____
2. _____
3. _____
4. _____
5. _____
6. _____
7. _____
8. _____
9. _____
10. _____

Students
Grades _____

1. _____
2. _____
3. _____
4. _____
5. _____

6. _____

7. _____

8. _____

9. _____

10. _____

Educators

1. _____

2. _____

3. _____

4. _____

5. _____

6. _____

7. _____

8. _____

9. _____

10. _____

Community Groups and Members

1. _____

2. _____

3. _____

4. _____

5. _____

6. _____

7. _____

8. _____

9. _____

10. _____

GUIDANCE AND COUNSELING PROGRAM OVERVIEW

National Standards Addressed

Categorize the standards addressed by the three areas of student development.

Learning To Live _____

Learning To Learn _____

Learning To Work _____

Subject Area Correlation

List the academic subject areas that are related to guidance and counseling program initiatives.

_____

_____

GUIDANCE AND COUNSELING PROGRAM OUTLINE

Month	Program Unit	Activities	Events
August			
September			
October			
November			
December			
January			
February			
March			
April			
May			
June			

Dear Colleagues,

Thank you for your recent responses to our school's Guidance and Counseling Program Needs Assessment. Your suggestions and comments have greatly assisted with our efforts to provide a comprehensive developmental guidance and counseling program for the students at our school.

Listed below are the needs that you have expressed along with those expressed by our students, their parents and guardians, and our community. An overview of this year's guidance and counseling program is also listed. Please contact me should you have any questions. Your support is appreciated.

Sincerely,

School Counselor

NEEDS ASSESSMENTS' RESULTS

Parents and Guardians

1. _____

2. _____

3. _____

4. _____

5. _____

6. _____

7. _____

8. _____

9. _____

10. _____

Students
Grades _____

1. _____

2. _____

3. _____

4. _____

5. _____

6. _____

7. _____

8. _____

9. _____

10. _____

Educators

1. _____

2. _____

3. _____

4. _____

5. _____

6. _____

7. _____

8. _____

9. _____

10. _____

Community Groups and Members

1. _____

2. _____

3. _____

4. _____

5. _____

6. _____

7. _____

8. _____

9. _____

10. _____

GUIDANCE NEWS
FOR OUR STUDENTS

Dear Students,

Thank you so much for helping me to plan our school's guidance and counseling program for this year. The ideas and suggestions that you wrote on our Needs Assessment are wonderful. Combining your needs with those of your parents, guardians, and teachers will assure that we will have an exciting program this year. Thank you again for your help.

Sincerely,

School Counselor

HERE'S WHAT YOU TOLD ME

Your Classroom Guidance Needs

1. _____
2. _____
3. _____
4. _____
5. _____
6. _____
7. _____
8. _____
9. _____
10. _____

Your Small Group Needs

1. _____
2. _____
3. _____
4. _____
5. _____
6. _____
7. _____
8. _____
9. _____
10. _____

HERE'S WHAT OTHERS TOLD ME

Needs of Parents and Guardians

1. _____
2. _____
3. _____
4. _____
5. _____
6. _____
7. _____
8. _____
9. _____
10. _____

Needs of Teachers and Staff Members

1. _____
2. _____
3. _____
4. _____
5. _____
6. _____
7. _____
8. _____
9. _____
10. _____

HERE'S WHAT WE'RE GOING TO DO THIS YEAR

Month	Classroom Guidance Unit	Small Groups	Activities	Events
August				
September				
October				
November				
December				
January				
February				
March				
April				
May				
June				

UPDATES FROM OUR COUNSELOR

Dear _____,

There is lots of exciting news about our school's guidance and counseling program. Listed below are just some of the activities for this (week, month, quarter…). Thanks to you and your support, we're having a GREAT school year.

Sincerely,

School Counselor

Classroom Guidance News

_____
_____
_____

Small Group News

_____
_____
_____

News About Activities And Events

_____
_____
_____

News For Parents

_____
_____
_____

News For Educators

_____
_____
_____

News From Our Community

_____
_____
_____

GUIDANCE HAPPENINGS

Edition Number _____ Date _____

For Students…

_____
_____
_____
_____

For Parents And Guardians…

_____
_____
_____
_____
_____

For Teachers and Staff…

_____
_____
_____
_____
_____

New Resources Available…

_____
_____
_____
_____

Community News…

_____
_____
_____
_____
_____

SECTION FOUR:
DATA COLLECTION & ACCOUNTABILITY

Section Four provides the busy school counselor with effective and easy-to-use forms for data collection and review. Additional forms are available to assist the school counselor with a practical means to report program outcomes and assure accountability.

These forms address the following areas.
- Program Initiatives
- Student Involvement
- Parent and Guardian Participation
- Colleague Participation
- Note Taking
- Evaluations
- Accountability Reports

Not only do these methods of data collection and reporting address accountability, they are also useful with the generating of positive public awareness and support for the comprehensive developmental guidance and counseling program.

DATA COLLECTION: PROGRAM INITIATIVES

Dates of Data Collection

Beginning Date _____ Ending Date _____

1. **Classroom Guidance Units**

   ❏ Name of Units and/or Sessions _____

   ❏ Number of Students Participating _____

   ❏ Grade Levels _____

2. **Small Group Counseling**

   ❏ Topics of Groups _____

   ❏ Number of Students Participating _____

   ❏ Age and/or Grade Levels _____

3. **Individual Counseling**

   ❏ Number of Students Referred _____

   ❏ Number of Sessions Conducted _____

4. **Consultation**

   ❏ Number of Parent or Guardian Sessions _____

   ❏ Number of Colleague Sessions _____

   ❏ Number of Community Sessions _____

5. **Workshops**

   ❑ Title of Workshop _____

   ❑ Audience _____

   ❑ Number of Persons Participating _____

6. **Referrals**

   ❑ Number of Referrals to School or District Services _____

   ❑ Number of Referrals to Outside Agencies or Individuals _____

7. **Special Programs or Events**

   ❑ Title of Program or Event _____

   ❑ Audience _____

   ❑ Number of Persons Participating _____

8. **Committees**

   ❑ Names of Committees _____

   ❑ Number of Meetings _____

Dates of Data Collection

Beginning Date_____ Ending Date_____

1. **Individual Counseling**

   ❏ Number of Students Referred _____

   ❏ Number of Sessions Conducted _____

   ❏ Issues Addressed _____

   ❏ Outcomes _____

2. **Small Group Counseling**

   ❏ Topics of Groups _____

   ❏ Age and/or Grade Levels _____

   ❏ Number of Students Participating _____

   ❏ Number of Sessions Conducted _____

   ❏ Outcomes _____

3. **Classroom Guidance**

   ❏ Name of Units and or Sessions _____

   ❏ Grade Levels _____

   ❏ Number of Students Participating _____

   ❏ Outcomes _____

4. **Special Programs and Events**

   ❏ Title or Program or Event _____

   ❏ Grade Levels _____

   ❏ Number of Students Participating _____

   ❏ Outcomes _____

Dates of Data Collection

Beginning Date_____   Ending Date_____

1. **Consultation**

   ❏ Conferences Attended _____

   ❏ IEP Meetings Attended _____

   ❏ Section 504 Meetings Attended _____

   ❏ Individual Consultation Sessions _____

   ❏ Telephone Consultation Sessions _____

   ❏ E-Mail Consultation Sessions _____

   ❏ Other Written Consultation Sessions _____

   ❏ Total Number of Parents or Guardians Participating _____

2. **Workshops**

   ❏ Title of Workshop _____

   ❏ Target Audience _____

   ❏ Number of Parents or Guardians Participating _____

   ❏ Outcomes _____

   _____

   _____

   _____

3. **Referrals**

   ❑ Number of Within System Referrals _____

   ❑ Number of Out of System Referrals _____

   ❑ Types of Referrals _____

   ❑ Outcomes _____

   _____

   _____

   _____

   _____

4. **Special Programs and Events**

   ❑ Title of Program or Event _____

   ❑ Target Audience _____

   ❑ Number of Parents or Guardians Participating _____

   ❑ Outcomes _____

   _____

   _____

   _____

   _____

5. **Volunteers**

   ❑ Number of Parent or Guardian Volunteers _____

   ❑ Categories of Volunteers _____

   ❑ Outcomes _____

   _____

   _____

   _____

DATA COLLECTION: COLLEAGUE PARTICIPATION

Dates of Data Collection

Beginning Date_____ Ending Date_____

1. **Requests for Services**

   ❏ Number of Students Referred_____

   ❏ Number of Requests for Materials or Resources _____

   ❏ Types of Materials or Resources Requested _____

   ❏ Number of Requests for Special Classroom Presentations_____

2. **Consultation**

   ❏ Number of Conferences Attended _____

   ❏ Number of IEP Meetings Attended_____

   ❏ Number of Section 504 Meetings Attended _____

   ❏ Number of Individual Consultation Sessions _____

   ❏ Number of Other Individual Consultation Sessions (E-Mail, Telephone, etc.) ____

   ❏ Outcomes_____

   _____

   _____

   _____

3. **Workshops**

   ❏ Title of Workshop _____

   ❏ Target Audience _____

   ❏ Number of Participants _____

   ❏ Outcomes _____

   _____

   _____

   _____

4. **Special Programs and Events**

   ❏ Title of Program or Event _____

   ❏ Target Audience _____

   ❏ Number of Participants _____

   ❏ Outcomes _____

   _____

   _____

   _____

5. **Volunteers**

   ❏ Number of Colleague Volunteers _____

   ❏ Categories of Volunteers _____

   ❏ Outcomes _____

   _____

   _____

   _____

NOTE TAKING

Remember: All counselor notes should be maintained in a safe, secure, and confidential manner.

1. Guidance and Counseling Activity

   ❑ Classroom Guidance Session

   ❑ Small Group Counseling Session

   ❑ Individual Counseling Session

   ❑ Student Observation

   ❑ Group Observation

   ❑ Consultation Session (Type _____)

   ❑ Parent and Educator Conference

   ❑ IEP or Section 504 Meeting

   ❑ Other: List _____

2. Date of Activity _____

3. Persons Present _____

   _____

   _____

   _____

   _____

   _____

4. Description of Activity _____

   _____

   _____

   _____

   _____

   _____

5.   Counselor Observations

6.   Additional Available Data and Information

7.   Counselor Recommendations

8.   Type of Follow-Up

EVALUATION: GUIDANCE ACTIVITY

Title of Activity _____ Date of Activity _____

Person Completing This Evaluation

❑ Student   ❑ Parent or Guardian

❑ Teacher or Other Staff Member   ❑ Administrator

❑ Other (Please List _____)

1. What are the strengths of this activity? _____

_____

_____

_____

2. What did you enjoy about this activity? _____

_____

_____

_____

3. Were there any parts of the activity that were confusing? If so, what were they? _____

_____

_____

_____

4. What suggestions do you have for improvement for this activity? _____

_____

_____

_____

5. Are there related activities that you would enjoy? If so, what are they? _____

_____

EVALUATION: PROGRAM

Person Completing This Evaluation _____

❑ Student   ❑ Parent or Guardian

❑ Teacher or Other Staff Member   ❑ Administrator

❑ Other (Please List _____)

Date of Evaluation

A. Program Planning

1. Have assessments been conducted to identify
   school and community needs? .... ❑ YES ❑ NO

2. Have the results of the needs assessments been shared
   with members of the school and community? .... ❑ YES ❑ NO

3. Is there a Guidance and Counseling Program Long Range Plan?..................... ❑ YES ❑ NO

4. Are there Guidance and Counseling Program Short Range Plans? .... ❑ YES ❑ NO

5. Are school and community needs addressed in the program plans?............... ❑ YES ❑ NO

6. Are The National Guidance Curriculum Standards for
   Student Development addressed in the program plans? .... ❑ YES ❑ NO

Comments _____

_____

_____

_____

_____

_____

_____

_____

_____

B.   Program Initiatives

1.   Does the program provide the following initiatives?
     Please rate them using the following scale.

0 = Is Not Provided	1 = Not Aware of This Initiative	2 = Needs Improvement
3 = Satisfactory	4 = Outstanding	

_____ a. Individual Student Counseling

_____ b. Individual and Group Student Planning

_____ c. Small Group Guidance and Counseling

_____ d. Classroom Guidance Sessions

_____ e. Parent and Guardian Consultation

_____ f. Teacher and Staff Member Consultation

_____ g. Parent/Guardian and Teacher Workshops

_____ h. Referral Services

_____ i. Guidance Related Materials and Resources

_____ j. Special Programs and Events

_____ k. Peer Helpers

_____ l. Mentors

Comments _____

_____

_____

_____

_____

_____

_____

_____

_____

2. Are there other program initiatives? If so, what are they? Please provide a rating for these as well.

_____

_____

_____

_____

3. Are there program initiatives that you would like to see included? If so, what are they?

_____

_____

_____

_____

4. What are the strengths of the school's Guidance and Counseling Program?

_____

_____

_____

_____

5. What suggestions do you have for improvement for our school's Guidance and Counseling Program?

_____

_____

_____

_____

6. What questions do you have regarding our school's Guidance and Counseling Program?

_____

_____

_____

_____

7. Do you have any other comments regarding our school's Guidance and Counseling Program?

_____

_____

_____

_____

EVALUATION: PRIMARY GRADES

Note: This evaluation can also be used as a needs assessment.

Name _____ Teacher _____

1. Draw a picture of how you feel when we have guidance activities in your classroom.

2. Have you been to visit with our school counselor? If you did, draw a picture of what you did and how it made you feel.

3. Draw a picture of things you like about guidance.

4. Draw a picture of things you would like to do in guidance.

ACCOUNTABILITY REPORT

Name of Counselor _____   School _____

Reporting Period _____   Date of Report _____

1. **Individual Student Counseling**

   Number of Students Referred _____

   Number of Sessions Conducted _____

   Baseline Data and Needs _____

   _____

   _____

   _____

   Outcomes _____

   _____

   _____

   _____

2. **Individual Student Planning**

   Number of Participating Students _____

   Number of Sessions Conducted _____

   Baseline Data and Needs _____

   _____

   _____

   _____

   Outcomes _____

   _____

   _____

   _____

3. **Small Group Guidance and Counseling**

    Topics of Groups _____

    Number of Participating Students _____

    Number of Sessions Conducted _____

    Baseline Data and Needs _____

    _____

    _____

    _____

    Outcomes _____

    _____

    _____

    _____

4. **Classroom Guidance**

    Titles of Units or Sessions _____

    Number of Participating Students _____

    Grade Levels _____

    Baseline Data and Needs _____

    _____

    _____

    _____

    Outcomes _____

    _____

    _____

    _____

5. Parent and Guardian Consultation

Number of Conferences and Other Consultation Sessions _____

Number of Participating Parents and Guardians _____

Baseline Data and Needs _____

_____

_____

_____

Outcomes _____

_____

_____

_____

6. Teacher and Staff Consultation

Number of Conferences and Other Consultation Sessions _____

Number of Participating Teachers and/or Staff Members _____

Baseline Data and Needs _____

_____

_____

_____

_____

Outcomes _____

_____

_____

_____

7. **Community and Agency Consultation**

    Names of Groups or Agencies _____

    Number of Sessions _____

    Baseline Data and Needs _____

    _____

    _____

    _____

    _____

    Outcomes _____

    _____

    _____

    _____

    _____

8. **Special Programs and Events**

    Titles of Programs or Events _____

    Target Audiences _____

    Number of Participating Persons _____

    Baseline Data and Needs _____

    _____

    _____

    _____

    _____

    Outcomes _____

    _____

    _____

    _____

    _____

    _____

PART TWO: ORGANIZING A COMPREHENSIVE FRAMEWORK

Overview

A successful school guidance and counseling program is anchored with a well-organized and well-planned framework. This framework provides the school counselor with the tools that are necessary to implement a developmental program that is both proactive and reactive to school and community needs. Part Two will assist the school counselor with resources that will create this necessary framework. It is divided into six sections. They are as follows.

- Referral Forms
- Appointment Reminders
- Small Group Guidance and Counseling Procedures
- Classroom Guidance Procedures
- Parent Conference and Consultation Procedures
- Intervention Management Techniques

Once an organizational framework is established, the school counselor will soon discover that program management is less time consuming. In addition, documentation of program initiatives will be strengthened.

TABLE OF CONTENTS

TABLE OF CONTENTS

TABLE OF CONTENTS

SECTION ONE:
REFERRAL FORMS

Section One provides the school counselor with ready-to-use referral forms that can be used by both students and adults in order to request responsive services provided by the school's guidance and counseling program. The referral forms are grouped into the following categories.

- Student Requests
- Colleague Requests
- Parent and Guardian Requests

These referral forms will assist the school counselor with the creation of a system that facilitates access to program initiatives by members of the school and its community.

STUDENT SELF REFERRAL
PRIMARY GRADES

Dear Counselor,

I would like to talk with you about something. It makes me feel…

_____    _____    _____

_____    _____

My name is _____ and I am in

_____ classroom.

84

© YouthLight, Inc.

Date _____

Dear Counselor,

My name is _____ and I am in

_____ class. I would like to talk with you about…

- ☐ Something that I don't understand
- ☐ Some good news
- ☐ How I can do better at school
- ☐ Something that bothers me
- ☐ A friendship problem
- ☐ Ways that I can help others
- ☐ Other: _____
- ☐ _____
- ☐ _____

Date _____

Dear Counselor,

I would like to schedule a time with you so that we can talk about
something that concerns me. My name is _____
and I am in _____ class. My concern is about

☐   Being a new student at this school

☐   Having to make an important decision

☐   Resolving a conflict with another person

☐   Something that disturbs me at school

☐   Something that disturbs me away from school

☐   Being successful at school

☐   Other: _____

☐   _____

☐   _____

Date _____

Dear Counselor,

I would like to arrange a time where we can discuss an issue that I have. This issue is primarily

☐ Personal

☐ Social

☐ Academic

☐ Athletic

☐ About my career future

☐ About my educational future

☐ Something else

Name _____   Class _____

Date _____

Dear Counselor,

I am interested in participating in one of the groups that meets at our school. My name is _____ and I am in _____ class. The group that interests me is:

- ☐ Understanding who I am
- ☐ Making and keeping friends
- ☐ Being successful at school
- ☐ Dealing with family changes
- ☐ Coping with a loss
- ☐ (Others may be listed here) _____

_____

The reasons that I would like to join this group are…

_____

_____

Date _____

I would like to refer the following student for guidance and/or counseling services.

Name _____

Class _____

The nature of this referral is…

❑ Self-understanding

❑ Social adjustment – peer relationships

❑ Academic concerns

❑ Grief and loss issues

❑ Others (please list)

This referral is based on the following observations and/or concerns.

_____

_____

The strategies that I have used to address this situation include the following.

_____

_____

I have notified the parents or guardians of this referral.   ❑ Yes   ❑ No

Name Of Person
Completing This Referral _____

Date _____

I would like to refer the following student for participation in a guidance program.

Name of Student _____

Class _____

I feel that this student would benefit from the following program.

☐ Peer Helpers

☐ Peer Mediation

☐ Mentoring

☐ Service Learning

☐ Small Group Guidance or Counseling

☐ Others (please list)

This referral is based on the following data.

_____

_____

_____

_____

The parents or guardians are aware of this referral. ☐ Yes   ☐ No

COLLEAGUE REQUEST FOR CONSULTATION

Date _____

I would like to request the following guidance consultation services.

☐   Assistance with a Parent Conference

☐   Information About Referral Services for Students and Families

☐   Assistance with a Classroom Issue

☐   Planning (Type_____)

☐   Assistance With A Student Situation

☐   Location of Support Resources or Materials (Type_____)

☐   Others (please list)_____

_____

_____

The request is based on the following needs.

_____

_____

_____

_____

A convenient date and time for me to meet is _____.

Date _____

I would like to request guidance and or counseling services for my child. My child's name is _____ and he/she is in _____ class.

The services that I feel are needed are checked below.

☐ Individual counseling (personal issue)

☐ Group guidance or counseling

☐ Academic assistance

☐ Academic and/or career counseling

☐ Referral for special services

☐ Participation in a guidance program (Type _____)

☐ Others (please list) _____

_____

This request is based on the following needs.

_____

_____

_____

I can be reached at _____ (address), _____ (telephone), and/or _____ (e-mail). A convenient date and time to reach me is _____.

_____

Signature

REQUEST FOR CONSULTATION SERVICES
PARENT OR GUARDIAN

Name _____ Date _____

Address _____

Phone (work) _____ (home) _____ (cell) _____

E-Mail _____

A convenient time to contact me is _____.

My child's name is _____.

I would like to request the following guidance consultation services.

☐ A conference with the school counselor to discuss my child

☐ A referral for special services for my child

☐ A referral for community services for me or my family

☐ Materials or resources regarding _____

☐ Others (please list) _____

_____

_____

This request is based on the following needs.

_____

_____

_____

_____

SECTION TWO:
APPOINTMENT REMINDERS

Section Two provides the school counselor with easy to use forms for helping students and their teachers remember guidance and counseling appointments. Please note that reminders should be sent in a timely manner. Those sent too early or too late may result in having students miss scheduled appointments.

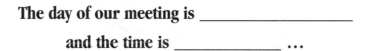

The day of our meeting is _____

and the time is _____ …

Date _____

Dear _____,

I am so looking forward to seeing you on _____

(day) at _____ (time). The clock printed above will help you

to remember our special time. Please let me know if you need to

make a change.

Take care,

Date _____

Dear _____,

This is just a friendly reminder about our upcoming appointment.
It is scheduled for

Date _____ Time _____

If for some reason you need to change our appointment, please let
me know by completing the form below and returning it to me. I
look forward to seeing you soon.

School Counselor

✂ -

Name _____ Date _____

I need to change our appointment. A better time for me is

_____.

Signature of Student _____

Date _____

This is a reminder of our upcoming appointment. I look forward to seeing you. If for some reason you need to reschedule this appointment, please complete the form below and return it to me before the date of our meeting.

School Counselor

Date of Appointment _____ Time _____

✂ -

Date _____

I need to reschedule our appointment time.

Name _____ Class _____

A better date and time for me is _____.

Date _____

Dear _____ ,

_____ in your class has an appointment scheduled with me for

Date_____ Time_____

I appreciate your assistance with helping the student to remember this meeting. If for some reason we need to reschedule, please let me know by completing the form below and returning it to me before the date of this appointment. Thank you again for your help.

School Counselor

✂ -

The appointment scheduled for _____ needs to be

rescheduled because _____.

A better date and time for this meeting is _____.

_____
Signature of Teacher

SECTION THREE: SMALL GROUP GUIDANCE AND COUNSELING

Section Three provides the school counselor with forms for organizing, managing, and evaluating an effective small group guidance and counseling program. The forms are arranged into the following categories.

- Planning
- Invitations to Students
- Letter to Parents and Guardians
- Monitoring

Along with the referral forms for small group guidance and counseling found in Section One, these forms will assist the school counselor with a systematic approach for creating, implementing, and assessing the outcomes of a successful small group initiative.

Name _____

Teacher _____

Please place an "X" beside the small groups you would like to attend this school year.

- ☐ Being A New Student at This School
- ☐ Making and Keeping Friends
- ☐ Understanding Family Changes – Divorce
- ☐ Understanding Family Changes – New Family Members
- ☐ Handling My Feelings When I Get Upset
- ☐ What Do I Do When Someone Dies
- ☐ Doing My Best With School Work and Tests

What are some other groups that you would like to attend?

_____

_____

_____

_____

_____

Name _____

Teacher _____

During this school year, students will be invited to participate in small groups in which they will learn more about a topic of personal interest. In order to identify groups that may be of interest to you, please place an "X" beside your choices from the list below.

☐ Being Successful in School

☐ Studying and Test Taking

☐ Being a Friend

☐ Being A New Student at This School

☐ Learning About Ways to Help My Community

☐ Becoming a Peer Helper

☐ Understanding Family Changes – Divorce

☐ Understanding Family Changes – New Family Members

☐ Dealing With Loss and Grief

☐ Understanding and Coping With Anger

☐ Dealing With Bullies and Teasing

What are the names of other small groups that are of interest to you?

_____

_____

_____

Name _____

Teacher _____

Students in our school have the opportunity to choose to participate in small groups that address individual or group issues and concerns. In order to select the types of groups that are of interest to the students in our school, please place an "X" beside the groups that are of interest to you.

☐ Being a New Student at This School

☐ Learning About Successful School Habits

☐ Dealing With Conflict and Anger

☐ What to Do When We "Break Up"

☐ Skills in Friendship Development

☐ Coping With My Parents' Divorce

☐ Dealing With Brothers and Sisters

☐ Being Part of a Blended Family

☐ Understanding Who I Am

☐ Becoming a Peer Helper

☐ Service Learning

What are some other groups that may interest you?

_____

_____

_____

Name _____

Teacher _____

Throughout the school year students will be invited to participate in small guidance and counseling groups at our school. Participation is strictly voluntary. In order to identify groups that may interest our students, your input is needed. Please take a few minutes to complete the following checklist of groups that may be of personal interest to you. Your assistance is appreciated.

I am interested in the following groups.

- ☐ Improving My Grades

- ☐ Dealing With Personal Relationships

- ☐ Preparing for Life After Graduation

- ☐ Handling Peer Pressure

- ☐ Getting Along With My Family Members

- ☐ Exploring My Career Options

- ☐ Coping With College Life

- ☐ Becoming a Peer Helper

- ☐ Dating: Sometimes It Makes Me Crazy

What are the topics of other groups that are of interest to you?

_____

_____

_____

_____

Title of Group _____

Age and/or Grade Levels _____

Time Allocations _____

Identified Student Needs

    1. _____

    2. _____

    3. _____

    4. _____

    5. _____

    6. _____

    7. _____

    8. _____

Legal and/or Ethical Considerations

    1. _____

    2. _____

    3. _____

    4. _____

    5. _____

Session Topics

    1. _____

    2. _____

    3. _____

    4. _____

    5. _____

    6. _____

    7. _____

    8. _____

Follow-up Strategies

1. _____
2. _____
3. _____
4. _____
5. _____
6. _____
7. _____
8. _____

Materials and Resources Needed _____
_____

Desired Outcomes

1. _____
2. _____
3. _____
4. _____
5. _____
6. _____
7. _____
8. _____

Methods of Assessment

1. _____
2. _____
3. _____
4. _____
5. _____

PROGRAM PLANNING – SHORT RANGE SMALL GROUP SESSION

Title of Session _____

Age and/or Grade Levels _____

Time Allocation _____

Legal and/or Ethical Considerations

    1. _____

    2. _____

    3. _____

    4. _____

    5. _____

Session Outline

  Opening _____

  _____

  Ice Breaker *(if needed)* _____

  _____

  Review Issues *(if needed)* _____

  _____

  Session Activites _____

  _____

  Discussion and Processing of Activities _____

  _____

  Closure and Follow-up _____

  _____

Materials and Resources Needed _____

_____

_____

Desired Outcomes

1. _____
2. _____
3. _____
4. _____
5. _____
6. _____
7. _____
8. _____
9. _____
10. _____

Methods of Assessment

1. _____
2. _____
3. _____
4. _____
5. _____
6. _____
7. _____
8. _____
9. _____
10. _____

Date _____

Dear _____,

I am writing to let you know that you are invited to join a group

of students who meet with me. The name of this group is

_____. We will meet

on _____ at _____ for _____ weeks.
    day of the week   *time*

In this group we will learn about:

_____

_____

_____

If you have any questions, please let me know. I look forward to our

first meeting.

Your friend,

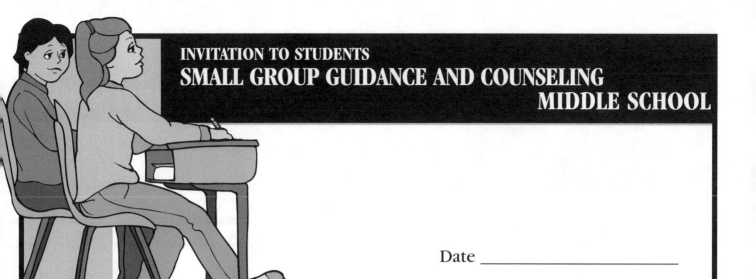

Date _____

Dear _____,

You have requested or been nominated to join a group that meets with

me at school. The name of the group is _____.

We will meet on _____ at _____ for _____ weeks.
                    day of the week   *time*

Our first meeting will be _____.

In this group we will explore:

_____

_____

_____

Please let me know if you have any questions. I look forward to our first

meeting.

Sincerely,

.

Date _____

Dear _____,

I am writing to invite you to join a group of students that meet with me at school to discuss and learn more about a situation or issue. The group you are invited to join is called _____.

In this group we will explore _____
_____
_____
_____

Our first meeting is scheduled for

_____. After that we will meet on

_____ at _____ for _____ weeks.
           day of the week   time

Please let me know if you have any questions about this group. I look forward to seeing you at our first meeting.

Sincerely,

Date _____

Dear _____,

Your child _____ has been invited to join a small group of students who meet with me to explore or learn more about a topic of interest. Your child's group in entitled _____.

In this group we will learn about _____
_____
_____
_____

The group will meet on _____ at _____

day of the week   time

for _____ weeks. If you have any questions, please contact me at

_____ or _____
telephone   e-mail

I look forward to working with your child.

Sincerely,

INDIVIDUAL SESSION MONITORING FORM SMALL GROUP GUIDANCE & COUNSELING

Name of the Group _____   Date of Session _____

Students Participating

Goals of the Session

Outcomes Observed

Counselor's Assessment

Follow-up Needed

GROUP EXPERIENCE MONITORING FORM SMALL GROUP GUIDANCE & COUNSELING

Name of the Group

Duration of Group (Number of Weeks & Time Allocations)

Students Participating

Goals of the Group

Issues Addressed in the Group

Outcomes

Counselor's Observations

Follow-up Needed

SECTION FOUR: CLASSROOM GUIDANCE

Section Four provides the school counselor with practical forms that can greatly assist with the development, implementation, management, and evaluation of proactive classroom guidance units and sessions. This section is divided into the following categories.

- Planning
- Letters to Students
- Letter to Colleagues
- Letter to Parents
- Monitoring

Combining these forms with the results of school-wide needs assessments will assure the counselor that an effective classroom guidance program will be established.

Name _____

Teacher _____

Please place an "X" beside the things you would like to learn more about this school year.

- ☐ Making and Keeping Friends
- ☐ Doing My Best at School
- ☐ Getting Along With My Brother or Sister
- ☐ Being Safe
- ☐ Feeling Good About Myself
- ☐ Work, Jobs, and Careers
- ☐ Thing to Do When I Am Bored
- ☐ Ways to Help My School and Community
- ☐ Being Helpful at Home
- ☐ Dealing With Bullies
- ☐ Moving – Getting to Know a New School and Neighborhood
- ☐ What to Do When Someone or Something Dies
- ☐ How to Handle My Feelings
- ☐ Being Healthy
- ☐ Other People and Countries
- ☐ Community Helpers

What are some other things that you would like to learn more about?

_____

_____

_____

Name _____

Teacher _____

During this school year, we will learn about many things in classroom guidance sessions. To help prepare for these sessions, please place an "X" beside the topics about which you would like to learn more.

☐ Understanding Who I Am

☐ Making and Keeping Friends

☐ Learning About Different People and Cultures

☐ Understanding Death and Loss

☐ Resolving Conflicts

☐ Being Successful at School

☐ Homework and Tests

☐ What I Want to Be When I Grow Up

☐ Ways to Help My Community

☐ Being Safe and Healthy

What are some other things that you would like to learn about this school year?

_____

_____

CLASSROOM GUIDANCE

Name _____

Teacher _____

During this school year we will explore many subjects of interest to middle school students through our classroom guidance program. In order to plan for this program, please place an "X" beside the subjects that you would like to discuss during classroom guidance sessions.

- ☐ Understanding Middle School Life
- ☐ Getting to Know Myself Better
- ☐ Dealing With Changes in Relationships
- ☐ Making Friends
- ☐ Understanding Different People and Cultures
- ☐ Taking Notes, Studying, and Test Taking
- ☐ Successful Work Habits
- ☐ Work and Careers
- ☐ Dealing With Peer Pressure
- ☐ Making Safe and Responsible Choices
- ☐ Understanding Changes in My Body
- ☐ Preparing for High School
- ☐ Community Volunteer Opportunities

What are some other subjects that you would like to discuss during classroom guidance sessions?

_____

_____

_____

Name _____

Teacher _____

During the school year we will discuss topics of interest to high school students during scheduled guidance sessions. In order to make these sessions helpful to you, please take a few minutes and complete the following needs assessment. Your assistance is appreciated.

1. What are some of the major challenges that confront students in our school?

   _____

   _____

2. What are the major academic hurdles that you face at school? _____

   _____

   _____

3. What are some issues and concerns that you would like to discuss during classroom guidance sessions? _____

   _____

   _____

4. How can the guidance program at our school better assist you with academic, career, personal, or social concerns? _____

   _____

   _____

5. What topics would you like to explore in regards to your plans after high school graduation? _____

   _____

   _____

6. Do you have any additional comments regarding our guidance program? _____
   If so, what are they? _____

Title of Unit _____

Grade Levels _____

Standards Addressed _____

_____

_____

_____

_____

Student Competencies Addressed _____

_____

_____

_____

_____

Subject Area/Standards Correlation _____

_____

_____

_____

_____

Session Topics

1. _____

2. _____

3. _____

4. _____

5. _____

6. _____

7. _____

8. _____

9. _____

10. _____

Materials and Resources Needed _____

_____

_____

Duration of Unit (Time Allocations) _____

_____

Desired Outcomes

1. _____

2. _____

3. _____

4. _____

5. _____

6. _____

7. _____

8. _____

9. _____

10. _____

Methods of Assessment

1. _____

2. _____

3. _____

4. _____

5. _____

6. _____

7. _____

8. _____

9. _____

10. _____

Title of Session _____

Grade Levels _____

Time Allocation _____

Standards Addressed

1. _____

2. _____

3. _____

4. _____

5. _____

Student Competencies Addressed

1. _____

2. _____

3. _____

4. _____

5. _____

6. _____

7. _____

8. _____

9. _____

10. _____

Subject Areas/Standards Correlation

1. _____

2. _____

3. _____

4. _____

5. _____

Materials and Resources Needed _____

_____

_____

Session Outline

Introduction _____

Participation and Process Activities _____

_____

Closure _____

Follow-up _____

Desired Outcomes

1. _____

2. _____

3. _____

4. _____

5. _____

6. _____

7. _____

8. _____

9. _____

10. _____

Methods of Assessment

1. _____

2. _____

3. _____

4. _____

5. _____

Date _____

Dear Students,

I am so excited about our upcoming classroom guidance session. Its

title is _____. We will

learn about many things.

Some of them are_____

_____

_____

_____

And of course you will help me learn many new things as well. I can't

wait to begin. I will be in your classroom on _____
                                                             date

at _____ . Please let me know if you have any questions. I'm
        time

looking forward to seeing YOU!

Your friend,

Date _____

Dear Students,

You are cordially invited to join me on an exciting learning adventure. Soon we will meet to begin an important classroom guidance session. Its title is _____.

During our time together we will _____

_____

_____

_____

Your ideas and suggestions for this activity are very important. Please let me know if you have anything to share. I will be in your classroom on _____ at _____ . I'm looking forward to
         date   *time*

our adventure. Take care and I will see you soon.

Sincerely,

Date _____

Dear Students,

I will be visiting your classroom soon to discuss something that I feel is important to you. The topic of our discussion will be _____

_____. I plan to be in your

classroom on _____ and _____ .
                      date   *time*

During our time together I plan to share the following information.

_____

_____

_____

Please be prepared for this meeting by_____

_____

_____

_____

Also, if you have any questions about or additional topics for this meeting, please let me know. I look forward to seeing you soon.

Sincerely,

Date _____

Dear Faculty and Staff,

One of the proactive strategies used in our school's comprehensive developmental guidance and counseling program is classroom guidance. I am writing to share with you some information about our classroom guidance program. Soon I will begin working with the students in your classroom on the topic of _____.

The outcomes that I anticipate from this experience are _____

_____

_____

_____

In preparation for this activity, you can assist me by _____

_____

_____

_____

Please feel free in contacting me should you have any questions about or suggestions for our classroom guidance program. Thank you for your continued support.

Sincerely,

Date _____

Dear Parents and Guardians,

Our school's comprehensive developmental guidance and counseling program provides support for our students in a number of ways. One of these approaches is our classroom guidance program. This program provides large group activities where students can learn ways to handle experiences before they become problems for concern.

I am writing to share information with you about our upcoming classroom guidance topic. Its title is_____ and its goals are

_____

_____

_____

You can extend and enrich the classroom guidance learning experiences at home by

_____

_____

_____

Please contact me should you have any questions about or suggestions for our classroom guidance activities. I can be reached at _____ or
telephone

_____. Your support is appreciated.
e-mail

Sincerely,

CLASSROOM GUIDANCE SESSION MONITORING FORM

Title of Session

Date of Session

Grades or Classess Participating

Goals for this Session

Issues Addressed in this Session

Outcomes

Counselor's Observations

Follow-up Needed

CLASSROOM GUIDANCE UNIT MONITORING FORM

Title of Session

Duration _____ (Number of Sessions) _____ (Time Allocations)

Grades or Classess Participating

Unit Goals

Strategies or Activities Used

Resources Used

Issues Addressed

Outcomes

Counselor Observations

Follow-up Needed

Suggestions for Change or Improvement

SECTION FIVE: CONSULTATION

An integral but often underutilized component of a comprehensive developmental school guidance and counseling program is consultation. Through consultation, the school counselor works with colleagues and parents and guardians in an organized approach for student support. Section Five provides the school counselor with consultation forms that invite and monitor other adult participation. The categories for these forms are as follows.

- Letter on Invitation to Parents and Guardians
- Letter of Invitation to Colleagues
- Letter of Invitation to Agencies
- Follow-up Letter
- Documentation

Through consultation the effective school counselor can increase support for the school program along with affecting positive outcomes for students and adults.

LETTER OF INVITATION–CONSULTATION
PARENTS AND GUARDIANS

_____
Date

_____
Name

_____
Street Address

_____
City, State, Zip

Dear _____,

One of the primary goals that our school and community share is our commitment to helping all of our students to be successful. Working together we can and do make a difference for our students.

I am writing to invite you to a meeting to discuss ways that we can work together to support your child,

_____. The meeting is scheduled for _____

at _____ in room _____. During our time together I would like to focus on

_____

_____

Please let me know what additional topics that you would like to include in our discussion. Also, please

contact me should you have any questions or need to reschedule our meeting. I can be reached at

_____ or _____.
      Telephone Number   *Email Address*

Your support is deeply appreciated. I look forward to our meeting.

                                        Sincerely,

Date _____

Dear _____,

I am writing to invite you to a meeting to review and discuss the progress and needs of

_____. The meeting is scheduled for _____

date

at _____ in room _____. The following people will also attend this

time

meeting. They are _____

_____

_____

During our time together we will address the issues of _____

_____

_____

Please let me know if there are other issues that need to be included. Also, feel free in

contacting me should you have any questions or need to reschedule this meeting.

Your support is sincerely appreciated. I look forward to our meeting.

Sincerely,

LETTER OF INVITATION–CONSULTATION
COMMUNITY AGENCY OR GROUP

_____
Date

_____
Name

_____
Title

_____
Organization or Group

_____
Street Address

_____
City, State, Zip

Dear _____,

This letter is written to invite you to a meeting to review and discuss the progress and needs of

_____.This meeting is scheduled for _____

at _____ in room _____ at _____.

Other persons invited to this meeting include _____.

During this session we plan to discuss _____

_____

_____

Please let me know if you have any additional topics for discussion or if you need to reschedule this meeting.

I can be reached at _____ or _____.
                   Telephone Number   *Email Address*

Thank you for your support. I look forward to our time together.

Sincerely,

CONSULTATION SESSION
FOLLOW-UP LETTER

_____
Date

Dear _____ ,

Thank you for taking time to meet with me on _____ to discuss the

progress and needs of _____ . It was a pleasure to meet with you.

As a follow-up to our session, I am writing to recap the issues that we addressed and the plans that we

made. During our meeting we discussed the topics of _____

_____

_____

We also developed a plan for _____

_____

Please contact me if I neglected to include any information or if you need to make any changes. I can be

reached at _____ or _____ .
                Telephone Number   *Email Address*

Again, it was an honor to meet with you. Your support is appreciated.

Sincerely,

CONSULTATION SESSION DOCUMENTATION

Date and Time of Session

Purpose of Session

Persons Attending this Session

Pre-established Goals for this Session

Issues Addressed

Session Outcomes

Counselor Observations

Follow-Up Needed

136

SECTION SIX:
INTERVENTIONS

Section Six provides the school counselor with necessary forms for developing, implementing, and monitoring student interventions. The categories included are as follows.

- Assessment
- Planning
- Monitoring
- Crisis Management Checklist

These forms will prove to be an important part of the school counselor's overall approach for providing responsive services for students.

In order to make an accurate assessment of a resistant student's behavior, an educator needs to gather as much information about the student as possible. "Leave no stone unturned" is a good motto. In reality, there may always be unknown and unseen variables in the life of a student that causes or contributes to the resistant behavior. Yet, the more information an educator can identify, the better prepared she or he is in making an informed assessment of the student's behavior. Sources of student data are a practical beginning for the educator who is gathering information. One may want to consider these data resources.

1. Permanent records

2. Attendance reports

3. Discipline records

4. Health cards or files

5. Individualized Education Plans (I.E.P)

6. Section 504 Accommodation Plans

7. National, state, and local test results

8. Report cards

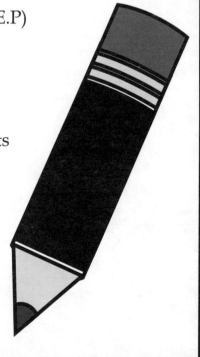

138

In addition, the educator on an information quest needs to consider the human resources that can provide additional information that is not maintained in written forms. The following people may be excellent sources for additional information.

1. Current teachers

2. Last year's teachers

3. Administrators

4. School counselors

5. School nurses

6. School social workers and psychologists

7. Parents or guardians

8. Child advocates

9. Peers

10. School bus drivers

Perhaps the following "fact sheet" can assist an educator in identifying the sources of student information and the results of the data collected...

Name of Student _____

School _____

1. What are my sources of written data to which I have access?

   _____

   _____

   _____

2. What are my human resources that can provide information regarding this student?

   _____

   _____

   _____

3. What have I learned about the student regarding...

   • grades and test results _____

   • abilities _____

   • attendance _____

   • family or community issues _____

   • health _____

   • relationships with others _____

   • self concept _____

   • behavior _____

An important consideration within the "information gathering arena" is the use of self-reports from students. Too often individuals fail to ask "the customer" to identify needs and concerns. An overlooked resource for gathering information is indeed the student in question. However, many resistant students are suspicious and/or threatened by the questions of adults when those questions are perceived as being either "too probing" or invasive. If this is the case, perhaps a subtle approach may prove more helpful. The following suggestions can assist the educator in gathering information from the student.

1. Have students write a story or draw a picture about themselves. In the case of the picture, have the students describe their drawings. One may discover new insights regarding the students based on these self-reports.

2. Conduct an informal conversation with the student. Perhaps you can talk during lunch period or recess time. Maintain a relaxed and informal situation. People tend to share more information when they feel comfortable and safe.

3. Conduct a personal interest inventory. This inventory may also prove to be a valuable tool for motivation. We will address this inventory again in Part Three. Here's a sample inventory.

Name of Student _____ Date _____

1. My favorite things include...

    _____

    _____

2. My special hobbies and interests are...

    _____

    _____

3. My friends include...

    _____

    _____

4. The things that make me feel happy are...

    _____

    _____

5. Things that frighten me are...

    _____

    _____

6. I become angry when...

    _____

    _____

7. At school I usually feel...

    _____

    _____

8. Away from school, I often feel....

    _____

    _____

Many students demonstrate resistant behaviors when they have experienced a significant personal loss. This issue is compounded when the loss is unknown or unsanctioned. When gathering information about a student, the caring educator needs to assess the possibility of loss issues or variables in the life of the student. As defined by Donna O'Toole in her curriculum *Growing Through Grief*, there are six types of loss that one needs to consider. They are as follows.

1. Relationship losses

2. External object losses

3. Losses within ones environment

4. Loss of self

5. Loss of skills or abilities

6. Loss of habits

Some losses are easily identified either because the student reports the loss or another person shares this information. However, there are losses that are not revealed by personal reports. These losses are only revealed through behavioral changes within the student. These changes can and do produce resistant behaviors in some students. Therefore, one needs to assess the behaviors of the resistant student in order to determine if a personal loss may be the real issue. The following checklist can assist you with this assessment.

Name of Student _____ Date _____

Responses To Grief and Loss

Which of the following responses does the student demonstrate?

Behavioral

_____ Crying
_____ Restlessness
_____ Irritability
_____ Sleep Disturbances
_____ Changes in Eating Behaviors
_____ Social Anxiety
_____ Withdrawal

Notes:

Physical

_____ Loss of Energy
_____ Shortness of Breath
_____ Sighing
_____ Dry Mouth
_____ Tightness in Stomach, Chest, or Mouth
_____ Weakness or Fatigue

Notes:

Cognitive

_____ Denial
_____ Disorientation
_____ Obsession
_____ Hallucinations
_____ Information Processing Disturbances

Notes:

Emotional

_____ Shock
_____ Numbness
_____ Sadness
_____ Anger
_____ Anxiety
_____ Fear or Dread
_____ Suspicion
_____ Guilt
_____ Loneliness or Isolation
_____ Helplessness

Notes:

144

According to the research of Fred J. Hanna (1996), there are seven precursors that assist people in changing behaviors. Often individuals do not change resistant behaviors into more positive ones because of the absence of one or more of these factors. The following table identifies these seven precursors. In making an assessment, educators need to review these categories and make note of the degree of significance they have in the life of the resistant student.

See table on next page.

Name of Student _____ Date _____

Precursors for Change

To what degree are the following factors present in the student's life?

Sense of Necessity	expresses a desire for change or feels a sense of urgency
Ready for Anxiety	open to experience or likely to take risks
Awareness	able to identify problems or able to identify thoughts and feelings
Confronting the Problem	courageously faces the problem and attends to issues
Effort	eagerly does necessary work and is cooperative
Hope	maintains a positive outlook and has high coping abilities
Social Support	has supportive network of adults and peers

From Fred Hanna (1996)

As a final component of the assessment process and as part of the concept of "Creating Support", the involved educator along with the support team is now ready to develop an intervention plan. Based on the information gathered and the intervention strategies identified, a realistic and practical plan can now be implemented. Please note that Section 2 will address a number of intervention strategies that can be part of this plan. A sample plan follows.

Name of Student _____ Date _____

Phase One: Current Scenario (Assessment)

Antecedent Event

Environmental and Social Factors

Current Behavior

Current Consequence

Phase Two: New Scenario (Intervention)

Environmental and Social Changes

Replacement Behavior

Reinforcement

MONITORING INTERVENTION PLAN

Name of Student

Date of Monitoring Review

Interventions Developed

Current Outcomes

Contributing Variables

Counselor Observations

Follow-up Needed

Comments or Suggestions

CRISIS MANAGEMENT CHECKLIST

Date: _____ Location: _____

Description of Crisis

I. **Immediate Response to Crisis**
- ☐ Basic Needs Provided to Survivors
- ☐ Gathering of Information
- ☐ Effective Notification and Rumor Control
- ☐ Hospital Accompaniment
- ☐ Media Management

Notes: _____
_____
_____

II. **Planning for Support Services**
- ☐ Identification of Decision Makers
- ☐ Involvement of Necessary Organizations
- ☐ Identification of Survivor Groups
- ☐ Initial Identification of Services Needed
- ☐ Scheduling of Support Services

Notes: _____
_____
_____

III. Crisis Interview
- ❑ Relationship Building
- ❑ Gathering of Information
- ❑ Assessment of Child, Family, School, and Community Issues
- ❑ Follow-up Debriefing

Notes: _____
_____
_____

IV. Identification of Treatment Issues
- ❑ Assessment of Physical, Emotional, and Psychological Needs
- ❑ Recommendations Identified
- ❑ Follow-up Debriefing

Notes: _____
_____
_____

V. Intervention
- ❑ On-site Crisis Intervention Provided
- ❑ Referrals Provided
- ❑ Monitoring and Follow-up Plans Developed
- ❑ Follow-up Debriefing

Notes: _____
_____
_____

VI. Follow-up
- ❑ Short Term Follow-up
- ❑ Long Term Review and Evaluation
- ❑ Monitoring for Post Traumatic Stress Disorder and Relapse
- ❑ Follow-up Debriefing

Notes: _____
_____
_____

PART THREE:
CREATING PROACTIVE SUPPORT

Overview

A hallmark of an effective school guidance and counseling program is its proactive approach in providing support for students, parents and guardians, colleagues, and the community. Not only does this approach prevent problems before they occur, it also builds understanding and respect for the total guidance and counseling program. Part Three will provide the school counselor with easy-to-use forms and letters that can be readily incorporated into a proactive program. It is divided into five sections. They are as follows:

- Affirmations
- Thank You Letters
- Reference Letters
- Public Relations Documents
- Bulletin Board Ideas

Using a proactive approach will greatly assist the school counselor with the implementation of a "person focused" guidance and counseling program. And in the end, is this not what we all desire.

TABLE OF CONTENTS

© YouthLight, Inc.

TABLE OF CONTENTS

SECTION ONE:
AFFIRMATIONS

Section One provides the school counselor with ready-to-use affirmation forms that can be used with any of the following groups.

- Students
- Parents and Guardians
- Faculty and Staff Members
- Community Groups and Members

These forms will help to "shed the light" on the effective activities, success stories, and accomplishments of members of the school and community. Using this approach, the school counselor can reinforce the positive outcomes created by others.

Date _____

Dear _____ ,

Today I caught you doing something WONDERFUL and I wanted you to know how much it means to me. Today I saw you _____

_____

_____

_____

_____

_____

_____

It is people like you that make this world so special. Thank you for being YOU.

YOU'RE A GUIDANCE
STAR

Date _____

Dear _____,

I just wanted to write you this note and say THANK YOU for your support of our school's guidance and counseling program. Your efforts are sincerely appreciated.

In particular I wanted to thank you for

_____

_____

_____

_____

_____

It's people like YOU that really make my day. Thank you for ALL that you do.

Sincerely,

156

© YouthLight, Inc.

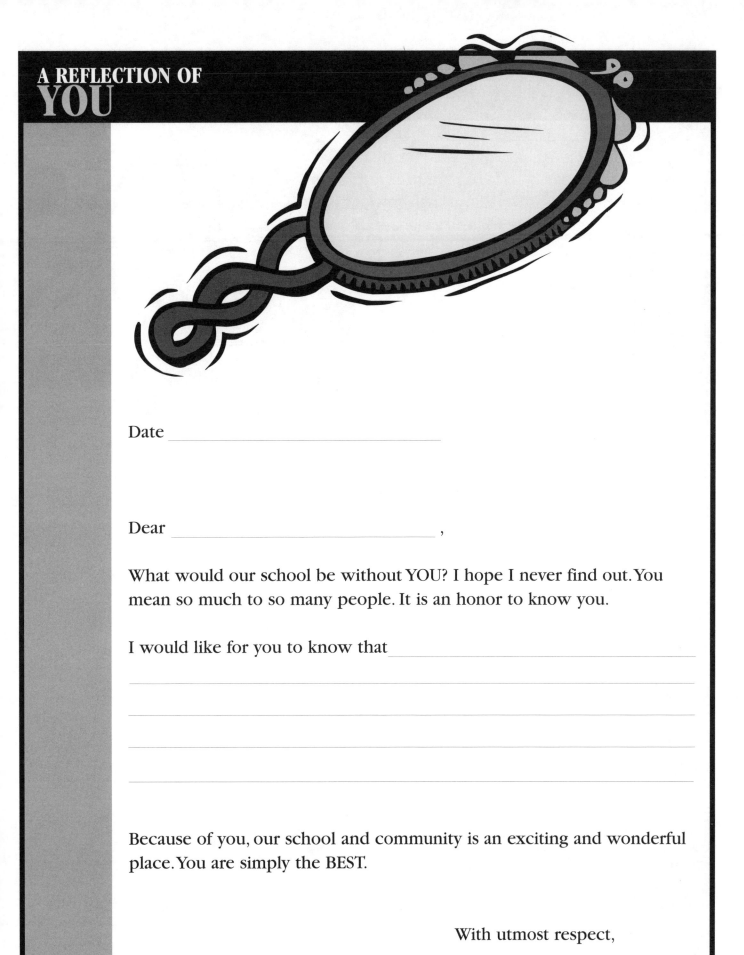

Date _____

Dear _____ ,

What would our school be without YOU? I hope I never find out. You mean so much to so many people. It is an honor to know you.

I would like for you to know that_____

_____

_____

_____

_____

Because of you, our school and community is an exciting and wonderful place. You are simply the BEST.

                                         With utmost respect,

HIP, HIP
HOORAY

Date _____

Dear _____ ,

I'm so excited to hear your wonderful news. I am thrilled for you. Please know that I share in this time of great joy.

I celebrate this important part of your life. It must be so affirming to

_____

_____

_____

_____

Congratulations!! I couldn't be more happy for YOU.

All my best,

Date _____

Dear _____ ,

I am just in awe of YOU. It is such a treat to have you as part of my life. Thank you for all that you do every day. But in particular, I want to commend you for _____

_____

_____

_____

_____

_____

Your positive energy lights up our school. You are so valuable to us.

Your friend and admirer,

YOU
LIGHT UP OUR LIVES

Date _____

Dear _____ ,

Who you are is such a gift to our school. You bring sunshine wherever you go. Thank you for being such an important part of my life. You are an inspiration to me.

Thank you for being _____

_____

_____

_____

Please continue to let your light shine. For in doing this, you bring such happiness to so many others.

You are a blessing,

AN "APPEALING" MESSAGE
FOR YOU

Date _____

Dear _____ ,

I just want to write you this note to say thank you for

_____

_____

_____

_____

I truly appreciate your kindness, dedication, and support. Knowing that you're here is such a comforting feeling. Thank you for who you are.

Sincerely,

APPLAUSE, APPLAUSE

Date _____

Dear _____ ,

You deserve a standing ovation! Thank you so much for your support of our school's guidance and counseling program. Working together we accomplish so much for our students.

I really want you to know how much I appreciate the fact that you

_____

_____

_____

_____

I hope you know how much I applaud you. It is a joy to have you as part of our school and community.

Sincerely,

THE BEST
IN THE BUNCH

Date _____

Dear _____ ,

You are certainly someone special to me. Thank you for taking the time to "go the extra mile." It means so much to our school family.

It is just wonderful to know that you

_____

_____

_____

_____

You are most definitely the "best in my bunch." And for that I am truly grate-ful.

Your friend,

A WARM FUZZY

TO

_____

_____
_____
_____
_____
_____
_____
_____
_____

FROM _____

YOU MADE ME PROUD TODAY

To _____

Because _____

_____

_____

_____

_____

_____

_____

_____

_____

_____

_____

_____

Your Counselor

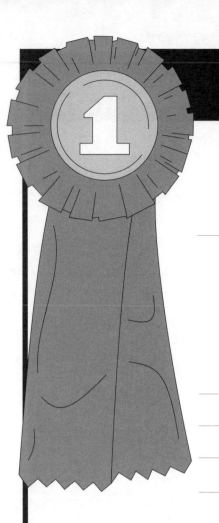

NUMBER ONE STUDENT

is a Number One student because

_____

_____

_____

_____

_____

_____

_____

_____

_____

_____

_____

_____

_____

_____

Signed _____   Date _____

THANK YOU FOR . . .
SHARING

Date _____

Dear _____,

I sincerely appreciate your taking the time to share

_____

_____

_____

_____

It means so much to us at _____ School to know that there are people in our community who will take the time to share their gifts with others. You are an inspiration to us all.

Thank you,

YOU ARE IMPORTANT

Did you know how important you are to me?
If not, then please let me tell you.

_____

_____

_____

_____

_____

_____

_____

_____

_____

_____

School Counselor _____

Date _____

KINDNESS AWARD

Congratulations ...

You are the winner of the Kindness Award because

_____

_____

_____

_____

_____

_____

_____

_____

_____

_____

_____

_____

Signed _____   Date _____

FRIENDSHIP
CERTIFICATE

Date _____

Dear _____ ,

You have been selected to receive this official Friendship Certificate because you are such a great friend. You are a friend because of these traits.

- Caring
- Considerate
- Kind
- Thoughtful
- Honest
- Loyal
- Trustworthy

In particular, you have been selected because you

_____

_____

_____

_____

_____

Congratulations on this much-deserved certificate.

Date _____

Dear _____ ,

I just wanted you to know that I am your friend. If there is anything that I can do for you, just let me know. It is our friendships that keep us strong and that help us to grow. Please know that you can always count on ME.

Sincerely,

WE MADE IT!!!!!!!

It's hard to believe but we made it. Thanks so much for all that you did. We couldn't have accomplished what we did without your dedication, talent, and hard work. Thank you for _____

_____

_____

_____

_____

_____

_____

_____

Please know just how much you are appreciated.

WELCOME ABOARD

Date _____

Dear _____ ,

I am so happy that you have joined our family at _____
_____ School. I can't wait for us to have the
opportunity to work together. I feel that you will bring many wonderful
gifts to our school. If I can help you in any way, please just let me know.

                              Welcome,

BON VOYAGE

Date _____

Dear _____ ,

I just can't believe that you are leaving us. Please know that you will be greatly missed. It has been an honor to work with you. I sincerely appreciate all that you have done for our school such as _____

_____

_____

_____

_____

_____

Please keep in touch. And remember that you will always have a home at our school.

Wishing you the best,

174

SECTION TWO:
THANK YOU LETTERS

Closely linked with affirmations, thank you letters provide the school counselor with the unique opportunity to express appreciation to those individuals and groups who have demonstrated support for the school's guidance and counseling program. Section Two provides easy-to-use letters that can be used to affirm the work of others. These include the following.

- Students
- Teachers
- Support Staff
- Administrators
- Parents and Guardians
- Volunteers
- Community Groups
- Career Speakers
- Other Guest Speakers

Incorporating thank you letters into a comprehensive school guidance and counseling program is not only a means of proactive support, it is a meaningful vehicle for positive public relations.

A THANK YOU LETTER
INDIVIDUAL STUDENT

_____
Date

Dear _____,

I would like to personally thank you for your support of and assistance with our school's guidance and counseling program. In particular, thank you for _____

_____

_____

_____

Please know how valuable you are as a student in our school. I am so thankful that you are here.

Your friend,

A THANK YOU LETTER
CLASS OR STUDENT GROUP

_____

Date

Dear _____,

It is indeed an honor to work with such an outstanding group of students. You are to be commended for a

"job well done." Your dedication and hard work are to be admired. Thank you so much for _____

_____

_____

_____

_____

Please know that I value each one of you. Your kindness and support means a great deal to me. Thank you

for being such an important part of our school.

Sincerely,

A THANK YOU LETTER
TEACHERS

_____

Date

Dear _____,

It is indeed an honor and a privilege to work with a professional of your caliber. Thank you for your support of our school's guidance and counseling program. Through your efforts so many students and adults will benefit. In particular, I would like to thank you for _____

_____

_____

_____

You are an asset to our school, our community, and our profession. Thank you for sharing your gifts and talents with others.

Take care,

A THANK YOU LETTER
SUPPORT STAFF

_____
Date

Dear _____,

Thank you for your continued support of our school and community. Because of people like you, this world is such a better place in which to live. Personally, I would like to commend you for your support of the efforts of our school's guidance and counseling program. Thank you for taking the time to _____

_____

_____

_____

_____

Please know that you make such a difference in the lives of so many people. It is an honor to work with you.

Sincerely,

A THANK YOU LETTER
ADMINISTRATORS

_____
Date

Dear _____,

I would like to take this opportunity to thank you for the support that you have provided for our school's guidance and counseling program. Because of your leadership, great things are happening. For this, I am truly thankful.

I would like to commend you for _____

_____

_____

_____

_____

Please know how much you mean to our school and community. It is my privilege to work with you.

Sincerely,

A THANK YOU LETTER
PARENTS AND GUARDIANS

_____
Date

_____
Name

_____
Street Address

_____
City, State, Zip

Dear _____,

Thank you so much for your support of our school and community. Because of your efforts, our school's

guidance and counseling program is able to _____

_____

_____

Please know how much I appreciate all that you do. In particular, thank you for _____

_____

_____

_____

You are such an inspiration to me. It is my honor to know you and your child.

With kindest regards,

A THANK YOU LETTER
VOLUNTEERS

_____
Date

_____
Name

_____
Street Address

_____
City, State, Zip

Dear _____,

It has often been said that "the best thing that one can spend on kids is time." That statement must have been said about you. Thank you so much for being a volunteer for our school. Your time, talents, and support mean so much to us.

I sincerely appreciate your help with _____

_____

_____

_____

Because of your dedication and enthusiastic support, our school's guidance and counseling program is able to provide the best for our students. We could not do this without you!

With sincere appreciation,

A THANK YOU LETTER
COMMUNITY GROUPS

_____
Date

_____
Name

_____
Organization or Group

_____
Street Address

_____
City, State, Zip

Dear _____,

On behalf of _____, I would like to thank you for your support of our

_____. Because of your efforts our school and

community will certainly receive many benefits.

Thank you for taking the time to _____

_____

_____

I am sincerely appreciative of your commitment to our efforts. Thank you for ALL that you do to make this world a better place in which to live.

Sincerely,

A THANK YOU LETTER
CAREER PRESENTERS

_____

Date

_____
Name

_____
Title

_____
Place of Employment

_____
Street Address

_____
City, State, Zip

Dear _____,

On behalf of _____, I would like to thank you for taking the time to share information about your career with our students. I have heard so many positive comments regarding your presentation.

Please know that many students will be helped because of the valuable information and resources that you shared. Our students will be better equipped to make informed career decisions. For this, I am truly thankful.

Again, thank you for taking the time to share your talents with us. We are truly fortunate to have career presenters of your caliber.

Sincerely,

A THANK YOU LETTER
GUEST SPEAKERS

_____
Date

_____
Name

_____
Title and/or Place of Employment

_____
Street Address

_____
City, State, Zip

Dear _____,

On behalf of _____, I would like to thank you for taking time to

visit our school recently. Your presentation regarding _____

was outstanding. I have heard so many positive comments regarding the information that you shared.

Please know that its people like you who are really making a difference in the lives of others. Thank you

for sharing your gifts and talents with others. It is indeed an honor to have your support for our school

and community.

Sincerely,

SECTION THREE:
REFERENCE LETTERS

Section Three provides the school counselor with sample reference letters that can assist students with their school, community, educational, and career efforts. These letters include the following topics.

- Award Nomination
- Application for School Organization
- Application for Community Program
- Job Application
- Post-Secondary Reference Letter

Through the use of reference letters, school counselors can greatly assist students with the attainment of their goals.

REFERENCE LETTER
AWARD OR SCHOLARSHIP NOMINATION

_____
Date

_____
Name

_____
Title

_____
Organization or Group

_____
Street Address

_____
City, State, Zip

Dear _____,

.It is indeed an honor to write this letter of support for the candidacy of _____

as the recipient of the _____. I feel that he/she is an

outstanding candidate for this honor.

I have had the unique pleasure to have known _____ for over

_____ years. During this time I have found him/her to be a truly remarkable student. In particular, I

would like to note _____

_____

_____

In closing, please know that I am honored to serve as a reference for _____.

Feel free in contacting me should you need additional information.

Sincerely,

REFERENCE LETTER
APPLICATION FOR SCHOOL ORGANIZATION

_____
Date   :

_____
Name

_____
Title

_____
Organization or Group

_____
Street Address

_____
City, State, Zip

Dear _____,

I am thrilled to write this letter of support for _____

application to become a member of _____.

I feel that he/she would make an excellent member of your organization.

It is my opinion that _____ possesses many of the talents and

abilities that would assure him/her success with your group. These include _____

_____

_____

Please contact me should you need additional information. And please know that I strongly support this

application.

Sincerely,

REFERENCE LETTER
APPLICATION FOR COMMUNITY PROGRAM

_____
Date

_____
Name

_____
Title

_____
Organization or Group

_____
Street Address

_____
City, State, Zip

Dear _____,

This letter is written in support of the application of _____

to participate in the _____. I have known him/her for

over _____ years and have found him/her to be a dedicated and caring student.

I feel that _____ would be an asset to your organization.

He/She possesses many talents and abilities that would assure him/her great success. These include

_____

_____

_____

I sincerely support _____ application. Please contact me should you

have any questions.

With kindest regards,

REFERENCE LETTER

JOB APPLICATION

_____

Date

_____

Name

_____

Title

_____

Organization or Group

_____

Street Address

_____

City, State, Zip

Dear _____,

This letter is written in reference for the application of _____

for the position of _____ with _____.

I am pleased to write this letter of support for _____ since I

have known him/her for over _____ years. During this time I have found him/her to be a dedicated and

responsible student.

I feel that _____ maintains many of the skills necessary to be

successful within your organization. These include _____

_____

_____

Please contact me should you have any questions or need additional information. I am honored to serve as a

reference for _____

Sincerely,

REFERENCE LETTER

POST-SECONDARY APPLICATION

_____

Date

_____

Name of Admissions Director

_____

Title

_____

Name of College or University

_____

Street Address

_____

City, State, Zip

Dear _____,

This letter is written as part of the application of _____

to pursue his/her post-seconday education at _____.

I am in support of this application for I feel that he/she possesses the aptitude, abilities, and maturity to be

successful within your organization.

During the past _____ years that I have been the school counselor for _____,

I have been impressed with his/her personal strengths. These strengths include _____

_____

_____

Please feel free to contact me should you need additional information. I am honored to serve as a reference

for _____.

Sincerely,

SECTION FOUR:
PUBLIC RELATIONS

An important strategy for the effective school counselor is the development of a positive and proactive public relations program. This strategy will significantly expand the awareness of and the support for the school's comprehensive developmental guidance and counseling program. Section Four provides the school counselor with "user friendly" forms and letters that can be used with public relations efforts directed towards school and community groups. Remember the old adage, "You only have one chance to make a good first impression."

This is a sample letter that can be retyped to include your pertinent information and then printed on school letterhead; or you may opt to copy this letter onto school letterhead and fill in the blanks with a pen. Remember to cover this portion of the letter and the title with white paper before copying.

SAMPLE PRESS RELEASE

For Immediate Release

Date: Name of Event:

Contact: Telephone:

_____ will sponsor _____ on

_____. A highlight of this event is

_____

In addition, it will focus on _____

_____

_____

Over _____ students, parents and guardians, and/or educators will participate. Anticipated outcomes include

_____

_____

_____

For further information, contact _____ at

_____   _____
Telephone Number   *Email Address*

GUIDANCE HAPPENINGS

Edition Number _____ Date _____

For Students...

_____
_____
_____
_____

For Parents And Guardians...

_____
_____
_____
_____

For Teachers and Staff...

_____
_____
_____
_____

New Resources Available...

_____
_____
_____
_____

Community News...

_____
_____
_____
_____

UPDATES FROM OUR COUNSELOR

Dear _____,

There is lots of exciting news about our school's guidance and counseling program. Listed below are just some of the activities for this (week, month, quarter…). Thanks to you and your support, we're having a GREAT school year.

Sincerely,

School Counselor

Classroom Guidance News

_____
_____
_____

Small Group News

_____
_____
_____
_____

News About Activities And Events

_____
_____
_____
_____

News For Parents

_____
_____
_____
_____

News For Educators

_____
_____
_____
_____

News From Our Community

_____
_____
_____

Date _____

Dear _____,

Your child _____ has been invited to join a small group of students who meet with me to explore or learn more about a topic of interest. Your child's group in entitled _____.

In this group we will learn about _____

_____

_____

_____

The group will meet on _____ at _____
                              day of the week   *time*

for _____ weeks. If you have any questions, please contact me at

_____ or _____
        telephone   *e-mail*

I look forward to working with your child.

Sincerely,

Date _____

Dear Students,

I am so excited about our upcoming classroom guidance session. Its title is _____. We will learn about many things.

Some of them are _____

_____

_____

_____

And of course you will help me learn many new things as well. I can't wait to begin. I will be in your classroom on _____
                                                                                    date

at _____. Please let me know if you have any questions. I'm
        time

looking forward to seeing YOU!

Your friend,

Date _____

Dear Students,

You are cordially invited to join me on an exciting learning adventure. Soon we will meet to begin an important classroom guidance session. Its title is _____.

During our time together we will _____

_____

_____

_____

Your ideas and suggestions for this activity are very important. Please let me know if you have anything to share. I will be in your classroom on _____ at _____.
                         date   time

I'm looking forward to our adventure. Take care and I will see you soon.

Sincerely,

Date _____

Dear Students,

I will be visiting your classroom soon to discuss something that I feel is important to you. The topic of our discussion will be _____ _____. I plan to be in your

classroom on _____ and _____.
                          date   time

During our time together I plan to share the following information.

_____

_____

_____

Please be prepared for this meeting by_____

_____

_____

Also, if you have any questions about or additional topics for this meeting, please let me know. I look forward to seeing with you soon.

Sincerely,

Date _____

Dear Faculty and Staff,

One of the proactive strategies used in our school's comprehensive developmental guidance and counseling program is classroom guidance. I am writing to share with you some information about our classroom guidance program. Soon I will begin working with the students in your classroom on the topic of _____.

The outcomes that I anticipate from this experience are _____

_____

_____

_____

In preparation for this activity, you can assist me by _____

_____

_____

_____

Please feel free in contacting me should you have any questions about or suggestions for our classroom guidance program. Thank you for your continued support.

Sincerely,

Date _____

Dear Parents and Guardians,

Our school's comprehensive developmental guidance and counseling program provides support for our students in a number of ways. One of these approaches is our classroom guidance program. This program provides large group activities where students can learn ways to handle experiences before they become problems for concern.

I am writing to share information with you about our upcoming classroom guidance topic. Its title is _____ and its goals are

_____

_____

_____

You can extend and enrich the classroom guidance learning experiences at home by

_____

_____

_____

Please contact me should you have any questions about or suggestions for our classroom guidance activities. I can be reached at _____ or
telephone

_____. Your support is appreciated.
e-mail

Sincerely,

SECTION FIVE:
BULLETIN BOARDS

An effective means for school counselors to enhance their public relations efforts is through the use of bulletin boards. Not only can they be used to publicize guidance and counseling program events, they can also be used as a proactive strategy for promoting developmental concepts. The following bulletin board samples provide the school counselor with blue prints that will support the overall success of the comprehensive developmental guidance and counseling program.

Directions: Place a "cut out" of the sun in the center of the bulletin board. Around the sun place "cut outs" of clouds. Label the sun "Guidance Happenings." On each cloud list and/or describe a guidance event or activity (i.e. classroom guidance unit, parent workshop, Financial Aid Workshop, etc.).

Classroom Guidance Unit

Parent Workshop

Guidance Happenings

Financial Aid Workshop

Directions: Place a "cut out" of a person in the center of the bulletin board. Next mount a number of hats around the "cut out." On each hat, list a role of the school counselor (i.e. listener, friend, career planner, etc.). Title the bulletin board *The Many Hats Worn By Your School Counselor*.

The Many Hats Worn By Your School Counselor

Directions: Cover the bulletin board with newspapers. Title the board *Look Who's In The News*. Now post articles about student accomplishments across the bulletin board.

Directions: This bulletin board can be useful in February during "National Random Acts of Kindness Month." Place a "cut out" of a rainbow in the center of the bulletin board. Surround the rainbow with "cut outs" of stars. Title the bulletin board *Our Random Acts of Kindness*. Encourage the students to write examples of acts of kindness from other students and place them on the stars.

Our Random Acts of Kindness

Directions: Place "cut outs" of a water spigot and a bucket in the center of the bulletin board. Next surround this with "cut outs" of drops of water. Title the bulletin board *Compliments Are Like Drops of Water That Fill Our Bucket of Kindness*. Encourage students and adults to write compliments to each other and place them on the drops of water.

Compliments Are Like Drops of Water That Fill Our Bucket of Kindness

Directions: Place a "cut out" of an exploding computer in the center of the bulletin board. Next surround it with "cut outs" of lightning bolts. On each lightning bolt list a technique for managing stress. Title the bulletin board *Don't Let The Stress Machine Get To You*.

Don't Let The Stress Machine Get To You